5 Easy Steps to

Make *your* Website your

#1

Employee

Advance Praise for *Five Easy Steps to Make Your Website Your #1 Employee*

This book gives you a series of practical, proven strategies and techniques to increase your web sales faster than you ever thought possible.

– Brian Tracy

Steve Johnsen's lucid, reader-friendly book shows you how and why your website can become your top employee....Don't miss this breakthrough book!

– Steve Chandler
Author of Reinventing Yourself

If you're ready to really make your website work for you, then read and absorb the strategies in this brilliant book by my friend Steve Johnsen.

– James Malinchak
Featured on ABC's Hit TV Show, "Secret Millionaire"
Founder, www.BigMoneySpeaker.com

When I first heard Steve speak on this subject, I was so impressed by his simple, no-nonsense approach that I immediately signed up for his boot camp. Then I ended up recommending his *Power Strategies to Make Your Website Your #1 Employee* boot camp to more than 4,000 of my friends and contacts. Now, finally, here is the information in book form!

In many ways, we have come full circle. Steve told me that he was inspired to write this book by attending one of my seminars, and I was inspired by Steve's message to make better use of my website to grow my business.

In *Five Easy Steps to Make Your Website Your #1 Employee*, Steve breaks down, in very simple steps, *exactly* what you need to do to make your website your number 1 employee. In other words, he tells you how to have a website that actually makes money for you. I highly recommend this book to anyone who has a business or a message that they need to get out to the world. Remember: You don't have to be good to start; you just have to start to be good!

– Joe Sabah
Nationally recognized speaker,
trainer, consultant, author, publisher
JoeSabah.com, SabahSpeaks.com and
SabahRadioShows.com

Steve Johnsen makes me look like a hero when he works with the businesses I have referred to him. His core values, his high integrity, and his wealth of experience set him far apart from other web developers. Steve gains people's respect and becomes a trusted advisor from the moment they see him in action. He loves to teach, and clearly explains how to make your website your Number One Employee. But on top of that he brings his clients clarity on where they need to go to operate a profitable business.

It is obvious that Steve really knows his field. He has been on the Internet since 1984 and has grown multi-million dollar businesses. But beyond that, people can sense how truly caring Steve is, and they really appreciate his simple, practical explanations of what used to be a complicated topic. His book is full of wisdom and teaches business owners how to have a website that really makes money for the business.

Steve regularly serves as an advisor to other businesses within our Make it Fly organization, and dozens of business owners have expressed to me how much they appreciate Steve's insights and wisdom. I strongly recommend Steve Johnsen and his book to help business owners with their business management and marketing challenges.

– David Block
Founder of Make-it-Fly

Steve has got to be *the* #1 expert on business websites. He has taught me a lot about the importance of your website and what it's doing for you, which is to make your business money. Finally, someone has actually explained all this mysterious technical "stuff" in terms that I can understand!

This book shows you, step by step, how to build a website that is strategic and makes your business money. The five steps are clearly laid out, easy to understand, and immensely practical. Steve's formula for website design, the "Cumulus Quattro," is absolutely brilliant. Every business should get a copy of this book.

– Tracy Dunagan
Founder of Impact Communications and
Your Business Writing

I can testify firsthand that this formula works. Steve's team did an amazing job putting together a website for us, and that website became our #1 employee. When the site launched, it was responsible for getting us more than a hundred thousand dollars in orders, and it helped our business make a quantum leap up to the next level. I would highly recommend this book to anyone who owns a business.

– Nannette Powell
Founder of Tweetie Pie Bags

Steve's *Five Steps* has definitely helped my business grow. Steve helped me figure out why my website was not producing—I was doing really well in the visual, verbal and functional departments, but some technical issues were holding me back from getting the leads I wanted. After Steve worked his magic, I began getting calls on a more regular basis. Don't just read this book—study it and apply it, and it will help transform your business too!

– Michael Grossberg
Spirited Images Photography
http://www.spiritedimages.com/

Steve, thanks for your contribution to the business community, especially through this book. Speaking from my years of designing and developing web experiences for clients, I can say you hit every important point and also caused me to resharpen my thinking. Every aspect of a website must behave purposefully. Your writing will help businesses focus on the aspects of their website that will provide a real return on investment.

– Dru Shockley
President & Founder, Call to Action Alliance Inc.
calltoactionalliance.com

In the Venture Capital world we're always looking for companies that have a solid marketing plan, and a great website is a big part of that picture. In *Five Easy Steps to Make Your Website Your #1 Employee*, Steve Johnsen breaks down the critical elements to creating a web site that works for you. Regardless of your marketing strategy, be it social media, email marketing or face-to-face, at some point all of your marketing efforts will lead to the website and that site needs to be able to move your clients and prospects towards the sale. In this book, Steve Johnsen demystifies the steps to making a truly effective site that gets the job done.

– Peter Adams, MBA
Author of Venture Capital for Dummies
Director, Rockies Venture Club
http://www.rockiesventureclub.org/

I can testify from personal experience that this works. My website sales went up 1000% after I worked with Steve. After reading this book, you will never look at your website the same way again. Steve draws on 20 years' experience in Internet marketing to craft the most enlightening and informative approach to designing a website that actually works; i.e., a website that actually makes you money. This is a remarkable book, written by a remarkable individual, and worthy of serious consideration by anyone who has or wants a website.

– Tom Ninness
Founder of Summit Champions and Author of
The 90 Day Journey to Your Sales Success
www.SummitChampions.com

5 Easy Steps to

Make *your*
Website
your
#1
Employee

Simple Tips to Have
Your Website
Actually Work for You to
Make You Money

Steve Johnsen, MBA

Centennial Publishing
Centennial, Colorado

Published by Centennial Publishing,
Centennial, CO 80112
www.centennialpublishing.com

Printed in the United States of America

Editing by Tracy Dunagan
Book cover design by Haniel Hann
Book design by Haniel Hann

ISBN-13: 978-1-63473-000-6

Library of Congress Control Number: 2014951905

10 9 8 7 6 5 4 3 2 1
First Edition October, 2014

With Appreciation

To my wife Esther, who has supported me 200% through all of my endeavors;

To my parents, who set a shining example and inspired me my whole life;

To my coaches and mentors: Gary Barnes, Steve Chandler, and James Malinchak;

To my good friends and colleagues, Haniel Hann and Tracy Dunagan, without whom I would never be where I am today;

To my children, who put a smile on my face every day and make it all worthwhile;

And to you, my reader…and the many clients I have had the honor and privilege to serve;

Thank you so much…for everything!

Table of Contents

Forward

by Gary Barnes

Dr. Ed Cole once said that "Expectancy is the atmosphere for miracles." I felt the same expectancy when I was reading Steve Johnsen's first draft of this book, because for the past few years I have had the privilege of having Steve as my coaching client, an attendee at my boot camps, my own webmaster for GaryBarnesInternational.com, and my friend.

A few years ago, when Steve was just starting his consulting business, he'd already had an impressive career generating millions of dollars in profits at a series of high-tech startups. Yet he was so shy about tooting his own horn to potential clients who could benefit from his expertise.

When Steve hired me as his business coach, I kept telling him that many people were selling "sizzle" to their clients; Steve really has the "steak," and it would serve people to deliver that steak. More than anyone else I know, Steve is truly motivated by a desire to serve other people in any way he can. His integrity level is 150 on a scale from 1 to 100. And when clients hire Steve, he really delivers, and delivers big.

Steve is naturally brilliant at what he does. When other people are focused on the artwork, or the bells and whistles, or the PageRank, or getting on the first page of Google for some obscure term, Steve has laser focus on what really matters: implementing strategies that grow your business. He truly does transform your website into your #1 employee. That's why I dubbed him, "The Website Income Strategist."

Everyone I know that has met Steve or had the privilege of working with him is amazed by the simple clarity Steve brings to the seemingly complicated world of online marketing. For the last 2½ years, I have been asking Steve every month, "When are you going to get your book out?" Now, finally, it's here. I hope you enjoy reading it as much as I have.

– Gary Barnes,
America's Traction Coach
GaryBarnesInternational.com

5 Easy Steps to

Make *your*
Website
your

#1
Employee

If I want something I've never had...
I've got to be willing to do something
I've never done.

– Joe Sabah

CHAPTER 1

Help!
I'm a Business Owner
and I Need a Website

Having a website has become a prerequisite for doing business today. However, for many small businesses, their investment in their website is not paying off. That's because it's simply not good enough to just "have a web presence" anymore.

> *You don't need a website.*
> *What you actually need is a profitable*
> *business. Your website is simply a tool to*
> *make your business profitable.*

As a marketing and technology consultant to small and large businesses, I would argue that you don't need a website. What you actually need is a profitable business. Your website is simply a tool to make your business profitable. So, if you invest in a website, the number one rule of thumb is to make sure it's a website that makes money for your business. And for your website to make money for your business, it must be working for you—and I mean literally *working*, as would your #1 employee.

What I found over the years is that many business owners have spent thousands of dollars on their websites. They've struggled and are hoping that somehow, magically, it's going to make money for them, and yet too often it doesn't do that.

You probably know someone who has a great product or service, but is currently frustrated that no one is finding them online. You may also know someone who has spent way too much money and time on their website, and then been disappointed that their site did not produce any results. Perhaps you have had similar experiences yourself. Now imagine: How would it be if your website were to actually become your #1 employee?

> *It is possible to build a website*
> *that actually grows your business.*

When someone starts a new business, one of the first things they usually do is have a website built. Then, they sit back and wait for the website to do something. The majority of business owners that we meet are still waiting for that to happen. Although this is a common situation, *it doesn't have to be that way!* It is possible to build a website that actually grows your business, and that actually pays you back, over and over again. In this book, I will show you exactly how to do that.

What is an employee?

When we say that your website can be your #1 employee, we are talking about investing in your business. Sometimes when a new business owner thinks about having employees, they think about the potential difficulties, management issues, or the costs. But experienced business owners know that a good employee can be a tremendous asset. Having an employee should be a revenue generator for your business. There is a rule of thumb that any employee you hire should generate value equal to three times their salary; for a sales or marketing employee that ratio should be much higher.

When I talk about your website being your #1 employee, I'm talking about someone who is working for you 24 hours a day, 7 days a week, 365 days a year, who never takes a vacation, never calls in sick, always has your best interest at heart, and is going to keep generating money for your business. One who is working hard for you to automatically bring you new connections, new business, new leads, new sales and new revenue.

No gimmicks

We are all very well aware that there are a lot of claims out there related to Internet marketing. I'm just as skeptical as you are about many of those claims. There are also a lot of gimmicks being advertised. I get emails every day promising to either help me make money in my sleep, or convincing me that somebody is going to put my website on ten thousand directories and I'm instantly going to be inundated with traffic. What I'm going to share with you in this book are not gimmicks or tricks, and they are not theories. I will only share with you tools and principles that I've actually used in growing multi-million dollar businesses. These are strategies that have actually

worked for me and for my clients, over and over again, and I know that they will actually work for you.

No jargon

Later in this book, we will cover some technical things that you need to know so that your website can actually become your #1 employee. However, I will explain everything in clear, simple language that is understandable and easily digestible.

High return on investment

In addition to a website being a necessary branding tool, websites can also be the most cost-efficient marketing tool for launching and growing a business. When you consider all the different ways you can spend your marketing dollars, some methods (like TV ads) require a huge budget, and typically have a very

---

No Short Bridges

For most small businesses, spending money on advertising is like building a 50-foot bridge across a 200-foot river. Yes, the big companies can advertise successfully, but only because their budgets are much, much larger than a small business's advertising budget. Make sure that what you invest your money in is actually going to work to grow the business.

---

low rate of return unless you have millions of dollars for a long-term campaign. Unless you are Coca-Cola or Budweiser, it's hard to make that work for you. Other methods have a lower cost and a higher rate of return.

A website, and more generally, Internet-based technology, is the most cost-effective method of marketing most small businesses, and usually delivers the best return on your investment. Not only can you generate more leads or sales with your marketing dollars when you invest in a good website, but also, the leads that you generate and the customers you bring in are more qualified. They have already stepped up and identified themselves as being very interested in your product or service.

In order to capitalize on this fact, the company or individual you entrust with the job of building your website must know *how* to build you a website that, first and foremost, makes your business money.

The challenges for small business owners are numerous, and one of the biggest headaches is not knowing where to turn when you need help building, evolving, or maintaining a business website. The industry serving small business web and technology needs is overflowing with information (and a lot of misinformation), competing messages, and lofty promises, and it's literally brimming with thousands of people who claim they can build a website. In the face of this madness, it's easy to forget to focus on *why you need a website in the first place*. A website is a marketing tool that helps you build a profitable business; it is a marketing tool with a purpose.

Many small business owners have been burned—numerous times, in some cases. Some have invested tens of thousands of dollars in websites that look pretty, but do nothing for sales. Some have invested very little, and ended up with a website that in no way captures the essence of the business and brand. They have paid hundreds of dollars, but in the end have accomplished nothing. Still others have ended up with a website that turns away prospective customers because it does not load or function properly. In essence, these people got less than nothing.

Another issue business owners face is that they don't know what they should expect to spend. Prices for building websites range from zero to the millions. On top of that, once a price point is set, they don't

understand what they should expect from the website, leaving them with no way to measure their return on investment. And, what about that dreaded term "search engine optimization," or "SEO"? Most business owners know they need it, but are frustrated because they have not had its attributes and value actually explained.
As a result, more than 70% of businesses are doing absolutely nothing to ensure their websites are being found….In other words, they are ignoring the need, in many cases, for a strong SEO strategy. No wonder so many websites are actually not getting found out in the wide, wide world of the web.

All of this has led business owners to frustration, disappointment, and lost revenue, and this is a major reason why four out of five new businesses ventures fail. It is time for small business owners to rise up and take action, and finally have a website that actually helps them grow their business.

The only reason
for having a business website
is to make your business money.

Your #1 employee

I believe the only reason for having a business website is to make your business money. Just like a good, hard-working employee, your website should be working tirelessly for you to grow your business. When you hire an employee, you expect that employee to work diligently to make you money. Your website should be no different. So what does a website do to make you money? To be effective, a website **must** accomplish the following three things:

1. **Present a professional, polished image and message to your prospective clients.**

2. **Get found by those prospective clients.**

3. **Convert those prospects into customers, making money for your business.**

I wrote *5 Easy Steps to Make Your Website Your #1 Employee* for one purpose: to empower you to strategically direct how your website is built so that it makes money for your business. In this book, you will learn the five easy steps that will solve many of the technological mysteries you've encountered…five simple areas on which you need to focus your attention when having your website built, so that it actually makes money for you.

There are myriad factors involved in Internet marketing, and it can seem overwhelming, but this book will demonstrate that it's actually not that complicated. The way in which all the elements work together is actually very simple, and is based in common sense.

You can—and should—expect your website to be your #1 employee. This book will show you how.

CHAPTER 2

Five Common Myths, and the Real Reasons You Need a Website

As mentioned in the last chapter, I strongly believe that the only reason for having a business website is to make your business money. There is a basic concept that most business people are familiar with: *return on investment.** Your website is an investment, and as such it should provide a return.

---

*Return on investment (ROI) means the benefit you gain by investing in something. If as a manager or business owner, you invest in something, you expect to get more than your investment back. If you invest $100, and get a benefit of $120, then you have gained $20 on your investment (20% ROI). If you get anything less than $100 out of your investment, that is a negative ROI.

The first rule in investing: don't lose any money.
The second rule: don't forget the first rule.

– Warren Buffett

A couple of years ago, I helped a publishing company with their website, on which they had spent more than $25,000 dollars. The site was actually very elaborate and quite nice-looking, but after all their time and money, the site was bringing in less than a $1,000 a year in revenues. Getting a few hundred dollars back from a $25,000+ investment is clearly a *very* negative ROI! The website actually took away from their bottom line rather than adding to it.

I'm sure you know someone who can relate to that situation. Like many people I talk to, the owners of that business were frustrated with their website, and could not understand what they had done wrong. Fortunately, we were able to provide a solution.

How did we help? First, we built them a new site, at a fraction of the cost of their original website. (The new website was different from the old website in a few fundamental ways, which I will mention a little later in the chapter.) Within a few months of its launch date, the new website had earned the company more than

$40,000. A few months after that, it had made more than $100,000 in revenue.

With some ongoing SEO work and a few changes in the products' pricing and positioning strategies, within about a year the website was earning more than $1,000,000 per year in revenue. In terms of ROI, the new site totally flipped the equation on its head. Instead of losing money on their website, this company was now making money—and making quite a bit of it! For a relatively small investment, they were getting a massive return—in fact, more than 10,000% ROI in the first year alone.*

How would you like to have an extra $40,000 in the next few months? Or an extra $1,000,000 per year?

The question I know you're dying to ask is, "How did that happen? What was the difference between the new website and the old one? What is the difference between a website that makes money and one that does not?"

---

*Just to be clear: Not all of our clients receive results as dramatic as this publishing company did. We generally take on projects where we believe our clients can achieve at least a 10x return on their investment. But, of course, no marketing program can have a guaranteed result, especially in the online marketing world where everything is constantly changing.

The difference in building a successful website versus an unsuccessful one doesn't, in reality, have to be that vast: however, the difference in results can be very significant.

One of the reasons the publishing company had struggled with their original website is that they had fallen for five common myths concerning websites. These are the five most common myths we have encountered in our work with literally hundreds of business owners and executives. In this book, we're addressing, and dispelling, these myths.

Myth #1: I need a website

The first of the five myths I'm addressing in this chapter is that which I discussed in Chapter 1: the belief that if you own a business, you need a website. Don't get me wrong—I'm not against websites. However, the problem with this thinking is that the website is **not** the end-goal; the website is a tool to help you reach the end-goal.

What you need is not a website. What you need is a profitable business. Your website is simply a tool to get you there.

When clients come to us saying that they need a website, our first question to them is always, "Why?" Why do you need a website? What do you want it to do? What business are you in? How is this going to help you grow your business?

If you aim at nothing,
you will hit it every time.

– Zig Ziglar

Once you answer those questions, you're on the path to understanding that a website is a strategic marketing tool which can be built to accomplish a specific business goal. It is only after that goal is defined that the website can be designed to accomplish it, rather than being built simply to "have a web presence."

Myth #2: Websites are expensive

The second myth that small business owners often hold is that *websites are expensive*.

As a consumer, when you want something, the important question is, "What is the cost?" Successful business owners have a different mindset. The question they ask is, "What will my return be?"

Here is a trick question that illustrates this key distinction: Which is more expensive, a $1,000 website that makes $100 a year, or a $6,000 website that makes $100,000 a year? Stop and think about that for a minute.

While the $6,000 website is a much larger investment, the $1,000 website is actually more *expensive*, because it's losing the business money. The $6,000 website has a much better ROI, and is therefore *less* expensive. If you could have a site that made you $100,000 per year, wouldn't you find a way to borrow the $6,000 to get it?

When business owners think that websites are expensive, this sometimes causes them to hold back from investing in a site that will provide huge value for their business. On the other side, it sometimes causes them to greatly overpay for a site that will not actually do much.

Ultimately, all business owners must think in terms of the return on investment: if I invest this money, what am I going to get back? If $6,000 will generate

$100,000, it suddenly becomes essential to invest that money. In other words, don't look at the price tag; look instead at the return. Smart business owners are constantly looking for ways to invest in their business.

Myth #3: Looks are everything

The third myth I experience constantly in my consulting work is that looks are everything. I do feel strongly that aesthetics are an extremely essential feature of most websites—the look of a website communicates your brand, your values, and your company's personality. Your website design can be a key factor in making customers comfortable working with you, and it can make you appear very professional. The world wide web is actually the great leveler. Because a website actually only consists of bits and bytes, with good design a new business on a small budget can look like a billion-dollar company.

With all that said, looks are not *everything*. In many important ways, the design of the website is as important to its function as paint color is to a car. It's not the paint that makes the car go fast. It is what goes on under the hood that matters.

In terms of what this means for a website, the technical and functional aspects of a website have a much bigger impact on its performance than the design. I have seen ugly websites that make a lot of money, but I have never seen a poorly coded or poorly functioning website that made very much money for the business.

The publishing company's first website (the one that was not earning them much money) actually looked very nice. It was built by a graphic designer who spent a lot of time making every page look great. The big problem, however, was that the pages were coded in such a way that the search engine could not read most of the content. Hence, the website could not show up in search results when potential customers were online looking for a solution.

Myth #4: We have to put everything on the site

The fourth myth I commonly hear is that *everything* has to go on the website. Companies, especially those that use their websites for retailing products, end up putting too much on the website: too much content, too many images, too many competing colors, too many different marketing messages, too many details…and the list goes on. The issue with doing this is that the purpose of the website becomes lost in the fray; if your website's purpose is to sell products, you need it to be clean-looking and simple to navigate.

The publishing company I mentioned in the previous chapter had hundreds of products in dozens of categories—but their original website had no search function and no easy way to navigate the categories. Although your first impression of the site was of a very nice visual design, it was nearly impossible for people to find what they were looking for!

On your website, it should be easy for people to find what they are looking for and take action to engage with you. They also must be able to find your business's phone number. This may sound trite, but many, many websites make it nearly impossible to contact the company because their phone number and customer service email address are buried amongst a barrage of information and imagery.

Have you ever been on a retailer's website to buy something and been frustrated by the checkout process? Have you ever gotten so frustrated that you changed your mind about buying from the company? On a retailing website, it should be easy for people to find products, continue shopping at various intervals, review their orders, check out, and pay!

The bottom line is, a website does not need to have everything on it. Rather, since your site was built to accomplish a specific purpose, it should be designed to make it easy for visitors to do just that. A cluttered website prevents customers from receiving the messages they need to receive, understanding the brand and why it's special, and easily navigating the website.

Myth #5: Build it and they will come

The final myth I see many people getting tripped up by is the, "Build it and they will come" philosophy. Again, this may sound like a statement of the obvious, but this is actually how most small business owners commission a website to be built. They hire someone to build them a website, then sit back and wait for something to happen.

This does not work for a new product invention. How do people find a product if they don't know it exists, much less understand what it can do for them?

This also does not work for opening a new business. Imagine what would happen if you built a new restaurant, hidden away on a small side street, and then simply waited for customers to find it, come in for lunch, and keep coming back.

The same is true for a website. Building and launching a website without a plan for getting traffic—no matter how great the site is—is like renting a new office space, installing a phone line, getting your business cards printed up, and then sitting at your desk waiting for phone calls. It just doesn't work that way.

The real reasons you need a website

Now that we've dispelled some myths, let's talk about the real reasons you need a website. There are three basic reasons why a website is critical for growing your business.

Image

They say image is everything. While that may not be completely true, a website is a critical component in creating an image for your company.

The business website is the first impression many people have of a company, and it is responsible for both building and sustaining your business's image. A business website should communicate, both visually and verbally, who you are, what you do, and what you stand for as a business.

A website can be very valuable from a credibility standpoint, which is critical for businesses today. Competition is fierce, and people have thousands of choices out there—and they are basing their choices, in large part, on the image a business projects. In fact, more than 90% of Americans today do not make a purchase without visiting a company's website.

I have talked to clients who did not have websites for their own businesses, yet they still were choosing and rejecting other vendors based strictly on how much they like the vendors' websites. In other words, they made big purchasing decisions based solely on the image presented on different vendors' websites.

Whether or not it is fair, the reality is that at least *some* of your potential customers will make their buying decisions based on the quality of your website.

A website actually levels the playing field between large and small companies. A small business will never be able to compete with a large, established one in television, radio or newspaper ads, in trade show marketing, or even in an expensive direct mail campaign. But, because a website is all digital, the small company with a smart website design can actually look better than the large business.

So, how do you build a good online image? There are many elements of a website that work together, such as use of color scheme, photos, artwork, and layout. Equally as important to a website's image is the copy, or content, that is used. The verbal content on a website is absolutely critical to the image you project: every word must convey strong messages that engage the visitor, keep him or her on the site, and, ultimately, drive that person to take action.

Get found

As previously discussed, no website—no matter how beautiful, functional or well-worded—will help a business make money unless people can find it! Herein lies one of the Internet marketing world's greatest mysteries: how do I build a website that gets found?

As you probably guessed, there are many components that must work together to ensure a website not only gets found, but also gets found by the right people. You've surely heard terms like "code," "HTML," and "meta tags" thrown around. And if you're like most small business owners, no one has ever really explained to you, in an understandable way, what these terms actually mean, and what to do about them.

There are a number of factors that play into this, which we will cover in great detail in Chapter 8. In combination, these technical considerations have a large impact on a website's performance, both in terms of user experience and search engine rankings, and especially in relation to who is finding your website. In Chapter 8, I will explain these so that you can finally understand what they actually are, and how they affect your website's chances of being found online.

Customers!

The end-goal for all businesses is to attract, retain, and grow a customer base. Maybe your business provides services or products, or perhaps it operates in a business-to-consumer or a business-to-business arena—regardless, all businesses need customers, whether you call them customers, clients, patients, or guests. Why invest even one marketing dollar if that dollar is not going to help you get customers?

When I say that your website can—and should—be your #1 employee, *gaining customers* is what I'm talking about. *That means your website must help you attract visitors, and then convert those visitors into customers.*

If you were to hire an employee for your business, you would expect a lot of them, would you not? You would expect that your investment in them would pay dividends to your bottom line.

Sometimes when we think about employees, the thoughts are negative: we think of employees as being difficult to manage, frequently a liability, or a straight-up cost. The truth is, an employee should be a revenue generator for your business. Any employee you hire should generate a value at least equal to three times their salary. And for a sales employee, that ratio should be much higher.

When you view your website as being your #1 employee, suddenly you are eager to make the investment. Your website—if built and managed properly—works for you 24 hours a day, seven days a week. It never takes vacation, calls in sick, or uses the training you provided to benefit a competitor.

Your website can—and should—gain customers for your business, and make your business more profitable. However, to perform this way, the website must be well built. Over the years, we have developed a simple formula for building a website well. Let's take a look at that formula in the next few chapters.

Men give me some credit for genius.
All the genius I have lies in this:
When I have a subject at hand, I study it
profoundly. Day and night it is before me.
I explore it in all its bearings. My mind becomes
pervaded with it. Then the effort which I make
the people are pleased to call the fruit of genius.
It is the fruit of labor and thought.

– Alexander Hamilton

CHAPTER 3

What *is* a Well-Built Website?

In Chapter 2, we talked about some of the myths associated with websites, as well as the real reasons a business needs a website. Now that we've established that a business needs a website for one primary reason—to make money for the business—we're going to closely examine the critical factors that must be considered in creating a website that does just that.

Having a website that is well-built is a mandatory first step in ensuring your customers find your site. And, once your site is found, it must convert visitors into customers. The success of a website is ultimately determined by its performance: it must work for the business, help the business grow, and make the business profitable.

In our role helping companies grow using technology, it is essential that every website we create is successful in this objective. A website that is well-built becomes an asset that pays you back many, many times over, and provides a foundation for ongoing business growth.

The Five Steps

Having built and optimized websites since 1994, over the years I have found that there is an important prerequisite to building a successful website. In addition, in order to be truly successful, the website must be well designed in four dimensions. Together, these five items—one important prerequisite and the four dimensions of design—constitute a five-step process for building a website that will actually make you money and grow your business. Every website that is truly successful in the marketplace follows this formula.

In order to ensure that every single website we develop is well worth the investment in it, and delivers the ROI it should, I developed a specific and measurable formula, which I will share with you in this book. This formula is rooted in these five primary steps. It is these five steps that make up the equation for website success. If your website is developed using this formula, it will literally guarantee that your website behaves as would your most valued employee!

Step 1: Purpose

The first step is actually a prerequisite for designing and building a website. Before beginning to develop a website, or any other marketing platform for your business, it is critical to define the purpose for it: what is the website supposed to do? How is it going to help the business reach its objectives? How does the website fit into your overall business plan and marketing plan? What is the key message you must communicate on the site?

The choice is yours.
You hold the tiller. You can steer
the course you choose in the direction
of where you want to be—today, tomorrow, or
in a distant time to come.

– W. Clement Stone

What I have found over the years is that many people have struggled to get a website built, and have spent thousands of dollars on it, hoping that somehow, magically, it is going to make them a lot of money. Unfortunately, it almost never works out that way, because websites are not mystic; just like anything else, they have to be purposefully built in order to accomplish anything. They must be deliberately developed to accomplish a specific, business-related goal.

Once you know your website's purpose, you can design the website to fulfill that purpose. The next four steps are the formula we follow for the actual web design, and they constitute the four dimensions of a good website design. A website that is built to accomplish a clear purpose and that is designed according to these next four steps will be a website that actually makes money for you.

You don't have to be good to start;
you just have to start
to be good!

– as quoted by Joe Sabah

Step 2: Visual

A website's design is often the focal point when a business is embarking on developing a new website, or enhancing and updating its current site. The fact is, the design of the website has a very specific *function*—in fact, many view it as an art (and I agree)—but a website is much more than good looks.

Every aspect of building a website should be done for one primary reason: to make that website do exactly what it is meant to do (to achieve its purpose). And to achieve its intended purpose, your business's website must have a graphic design that represents the look and feel of your one and only brand. Your site represents you on every page, so **every page is an opportunity to bring in business**.

The customization of a website design includes many elements, all of which are essential to the process of defining a brand; your brand, as represented on your website, is key to your business's success, both in the short- and long-term. These include:

- Capture your brand message, your positioning, and your company's personality.

- Communicate these elements visually, both with readily apparent and subtle/subliminal imagery.

- Warmly welcome and engage visitors, encouraging them to remain on your site, read about your product/service, and buy from you.

- Make visitors on your site feel at home, happy to be there, and happy to do business with you.

- Make visitors/customers appreciate the value of working with you.

Ultimately, the website's visual design must communicate your company's personality, and make people want to do business with you.

Step 3: Verbal

What you say on your web pages about your business and why it's special is critical to the success of your web site. A website that is written strategically will perform many essential tasks, including:

- **Engaging your customers**: People have short attention spans, so they must be engaged immediately upon landing on your website. When prospective customers or clients arrive at the homepage (or another page, for that matter) of your business's website, they must receive your message immediately; it must make them want to stay on your site to read more, or pick up the phone to call you.

- **Communicating your unique value**: Visitors to your business's website are looking for information on why you are different, better, newer, fresher, cheaper, and so on. The content on your website is responsible for clearly and succinctly expressing why they should choose your business versus your competitor's.

- **Causing visitors to want to do business with you**: What a prospective customer reads on your website is, in many cases, the direct cause of their next action. If you want them to do business with you, you must send precise messages that will *make them want to work with you…*messages that are *influential.*

- **Serving as a call to action**: The content on your business's website can be responsible for converting a visitor into a customer, which is the end goal. On the other hand, poorly written content (or content that makes no impact) can be the catalyst for sending them to a competitor's site.

The bottom line is, the content on your business's website should not just be good; it should be great.

Step 4: Functional

How a business's website is organized is a direct reflection of how organized the business is. When people have a hard time finding what they're looking for on a website, not only are they frustrated with the website, they are frustrated with the business.

The functional aspect of a website is of utmost importance to gaining and keeping customers. It is such a rudimentary expectation—that the website functions properly, allows visitors to get where they need to go, and permits them to do business with you—but unfortunately, this expectation often is not met.

The fact is, function can be overlooked by a business owner during the building process; there is often such a large focus on the visual aspect of a site that the functional element falls to the wayside. I have seen many cases in which business owners assume that the website will operate as it is supposed to, and they end up launching a site that loses them customers because the website simply does not work.

I cannot express this enough: *all websites should work*! There is simply no excuse for building a site that sends customers away because they receive error messages, or continually get sent to the wrong pages.

As with the other four dimensions of website success, all successful websites are built to accomplish key business and marketing goals, and their functionality is central to this goal becoming reality. Functionally speaking, a website must:

- Be easy to use!

- Be laid out in a way that gently guides the visitor toward taking the action that *you* desire them to take.

- Directly helps you grow your business by converting visitors into customers the first time they visit your site.

Step 5: Technical

The technical aspect of building a website is often the least understood, but it doesn't have to be. Yes, there are many, many technical nuances that, when properly developed to work seamlessly together, can make a very considerable impact on your website's performance. On the flip side, if these technical factors are not incorporated, it can mean the website serves no purpose other than sitting online with little to no traffic.

Everyone loves to spend time on a good-looking website, and an influentially worded website is certainly mandatory. The function of a website, as we discussed in Step 4, is essential as well, as is maintaining a laser-like focus on the ultimate purpose for the site. However, none of this does your business any good if no one can find your website!

That is why the fifth and final step in developing a website is so essential to its ability to become your business's #1 employee. In order to work for you, it must be accessible, and it can't do that if it does not get found in online searches.

A technically great website should be founded on solid market research, so that you know what your potential customers are looking for online; and, it should have each page built to be visible to your potential customers for the terms that *they* are searching for online. It should also be built with considerations such as code, page titles, and key words, because these all impact a website's technical performance.

To recap, the five steps in developing a successful website are:

1. Purpose

2. Visual

3. Verbal

4. Functional

5. Technical

The coming chapters will address each step in more detail, allowing you to finally take control and ensure that your business's website is working for your business 24 hours a day, seven days a week.

CHAPTER 4

Step One: Define Your Website's Purpose

As I discussed in Chapter 3, the purpose of your website—whatever that may be—is the whole reason you are having a website built. Therefore, you must clearly define this purpose before you begin.

The approach I've seen many people take with websites reminds me of a hunter out in the field trying to shoot his family's Thanksgiving dinner without aiming at anything: instead of thinking, "Ready. Aim. Fire!" he simply fires…but what is he firing at? That's not an effective way of tackling that turkey.

> *If I had eight hours to chop down a tree,*
> *I'd spend six sharpening my ax.*
>
> **– Abraham Lincoln**

It is this aim that I am talking about. We have established that your website is nothing more than a tool to help you build a profitable business. In your particular industry, what must you aim at if you want to become, and remain, profitable? Here are some additional questions you should consider when you're determining your website's purpose:

- What kind of business are you in?

- What kind of customers do you have, and are they looking for your product or service online?

- How are your prospective customers going to purchase your product or service?

- Is your market local, national or global?

Once you answer these questions, you will be closer to determining what, exactly, you are aiming at.

In a website project, we sometimes spend more time helping the client map out their marketing strategy than we do actually building the website. Yes, it's that important.

No horse gets anywhere until he is harnessed.
No steam or gas ever drives anything until
it is confined. No Niagara is ever turned
into light and power until it is
tunneled. No life ever grows
great until it is focused,
dedicated, disciplined.

– Harry Emerson Fosdick

The lighting designer

Many business owners go about creating their websites without thinking very deeply about this; for example, we were consulting recently with a woman who has a lighting design business. After asking her several questions, we learned that in her business model, she works almost exclusively as a subcontractor to general contractors—and we know that these general contractors are typically not searching for their subcontractors online.

Does this impact how we should go about developing her website? Absolutely. This woman's customers will indeed visit her website and evaluate her brand based on the image she projects and the influential information she offers on her site…but they are not likely to be *searching* for her online. Therefore, she should focus much more on the visual design and user experience than on any technical considerations related to driving traffic to the site. Her purpose is to convert clients who already know where to find her website, by presenting a strong brand on her web pages.

E-commerce with a purpose

We had another client that came to us to have her e-commerce site rebuilt. Through the initial consulting process that we bring all our clients through, we discovered that her dream was to get distribution in the major retail chains.

We built an e-commerce site for her that did in fact sell a lot of product, but that wasn't the goal of the site. The real goal was to get the buyers for the major store chains interested in her product.

With a clear goal and the right team working on it, we launched a website that got more than $100,000 in orders from national retailers within two months, and eventually landed her a licensing deal with Walmart.

Selective SEO

We had another client—a contractor—that had been spending money on SEO for two years… and had not gotten a single lead from his website. (Unfortunately, that's a common story that we hear all the time.) We were able to show him (and clearly explain) several "under the hood" technical issues that were preventing his web pages from showing up in search results.

However, during our initial consulting process, we discovered that he had a very specialized, niche service that he was offering, and one of the big costs in his business was filtering through the *wrong* leads that were generated from trade shows and advertisements. For him, five good leads were better than 100 unfiltered leads.

Hence, we crafted a very targeted SEO campaign to bring in a select number of well-qualified leads. Within 2 months of our starting to work with him, he had gotten dozens of good leads from his website, and has had more work than he can handle ever since.

Results are obtained
by exploiting opportunities,
not by solving problems.
All one can hope to get
by solving a problem
is to restore
normality.
Resources,
to produce results,
must be allocated to opportunities.

– *Peter Drucker,* The Executive in Action

More examples of clear purpose

Here are two more examples of websites that obviously reflect a clear understanding of their purpose. These are sites that are "done right."

The first is Dell's website. Dell, a multinational, Fortune 500 retailer whose bread and butter is PC sales, has developed and designed a website that makes it very clear that they sell computers, and that their products can bought online. It is also a breeze to navigate—whether I am a consumer buying a computer for my high school-aged son, a large enterprise customer buying a network system, or a small business owner looking for a lightweight laptop, I can quickly and easily find what I need, and make my purchase.

Dell made their website about convenience in shopping, and being clear about what they sell. The design is probably not going to win awards for creative artistry, but it doesn't matter, because the website achieves its purpose. The site certainly is attractive, but even if it were not, its ease of use would beat out an attractive yet difficult-to-navigate website any day.

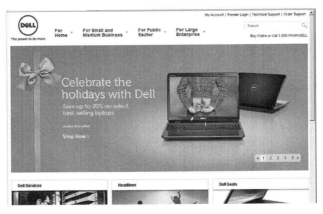

The other website I want to feature as one that was created with its clear purpose in mind is for a

© Andrew Gransden Photography. Used by permission.

solo photographer's company, Andrew Gransden Photography. In this scenario, the purpose of the site is to convince visitors that Mr. Gransden shoots beautiful photography in a variety of categories.

Because the product itself is so visual, the site was designed to showcase a varied portfolio of photographs, representing the different specialties the photographer shoots, as well as a rotating feature photo that dominates the homepage. Again, the purpose of the site is evident: when visitors see the actual product the photographer is capable of creating, they are influenced to hire him.

Action steps

Now that we have established the importance of purpose, it's time to put this into motion for your website. Spend about 20 minutes to undertake the following three Action Steps, and you will have accomplished Step 1: defining your website's purpose.

Ideas
are a dime a dozen.
People who implement them
are priceless.

– Mary Kay Ash

1. **Write it down.** Sit quietly in a chair with a pen and a pad of paper, and write down what you want your website to *actually* do for you in building your business. Is it to improve your image and promote your brand? Make people feel good about doing business with you? Help you build a list of people you can market to? Sell products? Generate leads for your sales team? Only after you have identified a business objective for your website related to making money for your business can you build the site to accomplish that goal. Try to limit yourself

to one primary, and, at most, two secondary purposes.

Primary Purpose:

Sell product

Secondary Purpose(s):

credability

Unique and educational

---

2. **Look at your website with fresh eyes (if you currently have a website).** Take a fresh, objective look at your website. Is your website currently designed to achieve the purpose you identified? It will also help to look at your own website from the user's perspective. If possible, get some friends

to sit down and browse through your website (without your help), and ask them to describe what they think the business will do for them.

3. **Measure success.** Decide how you will measure your website's success and put a program in place to monitor it. As an example, if you expect your site to result in lead generation, make sure you have a way to track where new leads are coming from (use a call tracking system or a separate phone number, special offer codes, etc.), and train your sales representatives to always ask, "How did you hear about us?" If the website is supposed to sell product, ensure you have a solid mechanism for tracking sales that result directly from website traffic.

Track Sales

CHAPTER 5

Step Two: Establish Your Online Brand Visually

In many cases when I first begin working with business owners, I find they are under the impression that the first step in building a website is creating a new graphic design. What I'm about to say may surprise you, but this is actually not the way I recommend that you go about building a website.

Why not? Because the visual design of a website must work seamlessly with the brand messages being conveyed. The visual design is a representation of what you are saying and claiming, and therefore, it is near impossible to effectively design a website before the content is written. However, once you have what I refer to as the "verbal" design—or content writing—

complete (which I will discuss in Chapter 6), you are ready to begin developing the visual design.

Your website's visual expression has a number of essential responsibilities, or jobs. These jobs are accomplished by designing a site that takes into consideration things like layout, color and graphics.

Remember your purpose

I'm going to return now to something I discussed earlier in the book, and that is purpose—your purpose as a business. As we dissect the elements of visual design, we still need to keep our focus on your ultimate purpose, or goal. Is your purpose to sell a widget? Or, is it to sell a high-level professional service? Maybe it's neither. Perhaps in your case, the purpose is not to sell anything outright, but rather to present a polished and professional image.

No matter what the purpose is, it must be identified…and the design must be created to help you achieve that purpose. One essential consideration in this regard is who your audiences are: What are they looking for? What are their expectations? What hardware and software do they use? What will they see (perceive) when they come to your website?

It is easy to become subjective when designing your business's website, but it is important to step out of your shoes, and into those of your prospective customers. These are the people who are going to make or break your business based on their reactions and actions upon visiting your website. Once you have determined the purpose and lined it up against an understanding of your customer, it is much easier to design a site in which all of the design elements work together to achieve the website's main purpose.

Visual branding

The second area of focus when embarking on your website's visual design is branding. A website is the first impression many people have of a company, and it should visually communicate who you are, what you do, and what you stand for.

Much of the branding comes from the overall design of your website…and, within the layout, there are a number of elements. Three easy to see layout elements that play a role in branding your business on your website are your color scheme, white space, and graphics (which includes things like images, photos, mastheads, and logo artwork). What do all of these visual elements suggest about your business? Are all the elements complementary? Or do they compete with one another, thus confusing the viewer?

The goal is for all of your visual elements to seamlessly create a strong image of what you do, what you offer, and what you provide. Ironically, a very common mistake represented on many, many websites is that the graphic elements do not work together to tell that story…so much so that the viewer is left with absolutely no understanding of what the business does (much less why that business is excellent or special).

Design considerations

As I just mentioned, design is a multi-faceted area of focus when designing a website. Although most people cannot consciously identify the reasons why, a good layout makes people feel comfortable with the website (and the company it represents), while a tightly packed layout makes people subconsciously uncomfortable.

A primary element of the effectiveness of a website's design is its **color scheme**. The fundamental use of color in any marketing endeavor is to help convey feeling or mood. For example, a mix of deeper blues and grays often is used to convey integrity; companies like IBM, Boeing and Chase—all whose purpose is to earn, and keep, their customers' trust— use these colors. On the other end of the spectrum, shades of red and orange are frequently used to get peoples' attention, to excite them: think about brands such as Coca Cola.

As much as the color palette is key—it must work with the graphic design elements and artwork to convey the visual impression you are aiming to convey—so, too, is the use of **white space** within the layout.

White space can be a tricky feature to manipulate when building a website, and yet the use of it is very central to the viewer's experience on your website. One of the most challenging aspects of white space is that the appearance of it can vary, depending on the size of the monitor your customers are surfing the Internet on.

For example, on larger monitors, white space can appear magnified, creating large border areas on the pages. Too much white space gives the appearance that there isn't much content on the site and therefore the site doesn't have much to say. Probably not the best approach, unless your name is Getty or Guggenheim, and you don't need to say anything for people to know who you are.

On the flip side, there is such a thing as too little white space. For example, when you look at the ads in a print newspaper, and see an advertisement that is overloaded with too much content, it might make you feel like there is too much to read, so therefore you do not read it. This is due to a *lack* of white space.

In reality, one of the intended functions of white space on a website might be referred to as breathing space. Fortunately, good website designers understand this delicate balance. They will ensure there are sufficient, yet not overly large, margins on the top, bottom, and sides. They will also consider and manipulate the space between the lines of text—the greater the space, the more breathing room. (Note that this space is directly impacted by the typeface chosen and point size used, which are additional elements of a good website design.)

Breathing room, however, is not the only function, or even the primary function of white space. White space is also about directing the viewer's attention. That's why museums use large amounts of white space to focus your attention onto a very tiny block of text. A good designer will use white space in creative ways that most of us would never think of.

Layout—Images, artwork, graphic design elements

Photos, drawings and other graphic artwork are essential ingredients for most websites, and they all have several different uses in design. The most basic way to describe their function is that they are there to tell a story. A carefully chosen photo or visual can do wonders to help establish brand identity and product identity.

The tricky aspect of a graphic such as a photo is that it is part of the content or material that needs to be *designed into* the website. The shape, content and size of an image all affect the impact of the page; since all the graphic elements on the page work together, they all need to be carefully considered by a designer so that the end result has a strong and lasting impact on the reader.

Many times people ask if I can "drop in" a photo or graphic here or there, and what I have just explained is the reason that the answer is not always yes. In order to make the right impression on the viewer, any and all graphic elements must be looked at as puzzle pieces. Alone, they do not do anything visually; together, they embody an image that tells a story.

There are also a number of secondary uses of smaller photos and visual aspects. One of the most important is to help draw the readers' eyes across the page (combined with the skilled use of white space). The objective of your website design is to keep the reader on it, and direct their attention to the call to action (common calls to action are to contact you, make a purchase, or click a link).

When designed properly, the graphics, color scheme and layout will draw the viewers' eyes to the intended areas of the site. When not designed properly, elements like these will distract a reader, or, even worse, lead them away from your message and site.

Now I would like to offer a demonstration of a visual website design that I view as not having been done correctly. I did not get permission to include the home page here, but you can view it at this link: www. kidsastronomy.com. The home page for this website has elements all over the page which are competing with one another. There is no consistency among colors or design elements, and yet no one particular thing stands out, either. There are a lot of sharp edges and overlapping images, which make the website's appearance that of an amateur. When I look at this site, as the user, I do not know what to do, where to go, or what I might find.

The next website is not very attractive, either. I would not classify it as ugly, per se, but it is certainly not pleasing to the eye. It is very obviously a templated site; all the elements look thrown together, and there appears to have been no real effort to provide a consistent look and make the design aspects work together.

As I said before, the design is not blatantly unattractive, but it does not communicate anything concerning the company's personality. It does not represent the company's product or value proposition. It also lacks proper typography and text formatting, which suggests it was built by an amateur designer who most likely haphazardly grabbed and used a template, without much thought.

Now let's take a look at several websites that were designed very effectively.

Make it in Modeling

A good visual design establishes instant credibility, and you can tell at a glance what the site is all about. This website certainly achieves that goal. The colors, the layout, and the images all work together to instantly communicate that here is a successful professional model who can teach you how to make it in the same field.

Design © 2009 BluReel Inc. Used by permission. All rights reserved.

Say Cheese!

Here is another site with a strong design that instantly establishes credibility. At one glance, you know what the company does, and that they do it very well.

Design © 2013 BluReel Inc. Used by permission. All rights reserved.

Label printer

This design was created for a company that prints labels for commercial products. You will notice that the website design itself looks like a label (the product the company sells), and also conveys an image of high-class quality.

On this website, the colors, images and layout work seamlessly together, and the perception when looking at the site is that it is a cohesive whole. Additionally, it is quite obvious the text has been professionally formatted by a graphic artist who understands typography.

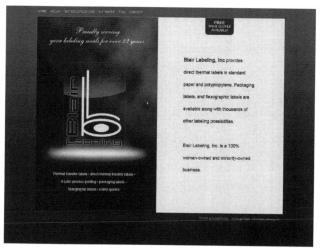

Design © 2011 Cumulus Consulting. All rights reserved.

Auctioneer

This site is for an auctioneer that produces charity events. The entire site design makes it look like Brad is on stage. Brad's logo is suggestive of the audio production that he includes with his auctioneering, and the quality of the site design makes him stand head and shoulders above all of his competition.

Design © 2012 Cumulus Consulting. All rights reserved.

Action steps

Now that we have examined some of the more important categories of consideration when looking at a website's visual design, it's time to take some action.

Your brand's entire look, from logos to business cards to the website, should consistently communicate your brand's personality. In order to ensure your website is doing its job in this regard, ask and answer the following questions for yourself, in writing.

- Do you know what your brand personality IS that you're trying to communicate? If so, write it down. If not, consider: what does your company stand for (or, what do you want it to stand for?)

- Were your graphics professionally designed by someone who understands branding? Or were they designed by a production graphic artist? If there was not a branding expert involved, you will want to bring someone to the table who understands both.

A website that has an effective and attractive visual design is truly rare these days. That is because most businesses do not ask themselves the questions presented in this chapter...nor do they understand the delicate balance of elements presented here.

Once you grasp how these subtle yet essential elements work together, you are ready to move forward on developing your vision for your website's graphic design.

Eco, organic, no syn preservatives.

CHAPTER 6

Step Three: Write Influential Content

As I mentioned in the previous chapter, the verbal content you create describes your brand and why it is special—and this leads the whole process of building a website. This is because until you know who you are and what makes you excellent—and state it in words—you cannot do a good job of painting a visual picture that enhances it.

In the user's experience, the visual design is the first impression they have of the website, but the verbal design (the "copy," or content) is what will actually compel them to take action. However, in building the site, it is hard to create the visual design without first having good copy in hand, because both the visual and verbal design should work together to deliver a consistent message.

> *The difference between the right word and an*
> *almost-right word is the difference between*
> *lightning and a lightning bug.*
>
> **– Mark Twain**

The bottom line is that if a website is going to be good, it must be well designed verbally. This is because professionally written copy has immeasurable value. It demonstrates where you are exceptional; it engages your customers; it clearly communicates your value. And good copy causes the visitors to your website to want to do business with you. Beyond that, great content ensures that what your prospective customers read starts the conversion process—it takes them from being curious to being convinced.

Built on your key messages

Just as a good visual design is created to convey a message (rather than merely "looking nice"), good copy should also be written around your key marketing messages. *Key messages* are a short list of simple yet unique points that you will make throughout all of your communications. They are usually written to emphasize your positioning, as well as the special and unique value that you offer to customers. They are the points you absolutely want your customers and potential customers to remember.

For example, one of our key messages is "Make your website your #1 employee."™ Since it is built into all of our communications, it has become our trademark phrase.

If you have never taken the time to develop key marketing messages for your business, you might want to do that now, or even better, you might want to hire a PR/marketing strategy expert to help you do so. Your key messages will then become a key part of your larger communication plan.

Outside eyes

Writing good copy is one of the most important—and the most difficult—steps in building a website that makes money for your business. It is even more difficult to write copy for yourself. This is even true for many copy writers that I know! There is something about having a set of outside eyes that enables us to take our copy up to another level. We strongly recommend to all our clients that they have an outside expert help them with their copy.

Depth of understanding

Both your designer (visual) and copy writer (verbal) should spend a significant amount of time understanding your business and your industry, so that they can create a website that communicates your business's personality and value. Once again, it's not just about "sounding good," but about having copy that communicates your unique message and value that will get people to take action.

Critical areas to consider

There are five critical areas to address when developing website content. All five must be considered as you go about building or updating your website, and before you put pen to paper.

1. Know what you want

The results you get from your website are often a direct response to the words you use and the messages you convey…so, you need to know what your goals are, both short and long term. More simply put, **know what you want**.

For example, today you may want to make sales, but three years down the road, maybe you want to sell your business. Or, today you may be launching a business, but a year from now you aim to add a new product line. Maybe you are trying to build credibility as an expert in your field, to build a reputation for yourself and your brand.

All of these objectives are essential to define before you write your content. Think about it: even if you were writing content for a website to sell your personal attributes, you would have to know what you are wanting in the end.

2. Know what you bring

The second rule of thumb in creating great content is, **know what you bring**. A good majority of business owners feel like salespeople at all times. Certainly, sales are essential for a business to succeed; however, sometimes you need to step away and realize that while you are indeed *asking* customers for business what is more important is that you are *offering* them something of value.

This new focus actually encourages you to think differently. When you believe in, and are focused on, your unique value, your message changes; it is more convincing. These considerations will drive your content; when you believe you are an asset, your message becomes extremely influential, because now you are creating content that's really true.

3. Know your audience

Even though I'm addressing 'audience' as the third area of critical consideration, I actually believe it is the most important. The simple fact here is, it is not worth putting anything down on paper if you don't know or understand who your intended reader is.

Many times in business, we get caught up in the "how" of everything: how to market, how to sell, how to make money, how to manage…the list goes on. How many times do we step back and focus on the "who?"

These "who" are your bread and butter, so you must determine who your "who" are, get to know them, and come to understand their likes and dislikes: the things that drive them and the things that deter them. Because ultimately, you must know what your audience wants. After all, how can you convince someone you have what they want, if you don't even know what it is they want, and why they want it?

So, make sure you spend time studying your audiences. Define the specific characteristics of these audiences. For example, if you decide that your audience consists of working moms in Chicago, what are some of the characteristics this demographic group typically shares? Let's say that your ideal customer demographic is mid-sized law firms: what do you provide for them? Do they have common burdens that your business relieves?

The bottom line is, regardless of who your audience is, what they care about most is what's in it for them. It may sound somewhat callous, but if you always remember what they care about—and communicate to them in a way that convinces them you will give them what they need and want—you are much closer to having truly effective content.

4. Tell a story

As business owners, we have our own agendas. Because of this, many times a business owner will create marketing or branding content from that angle…we are still thinking, "how can I get them to buy?" versus "what's really in it for my customer?" This perspective will make a business owner seem pushy and uncaring.

One surefire way to avoid coming across as pushy in messaging is to focus on storytelling. Yes, it might sound strange, but people love stories! As a customer of any service or product, if I am told a story, I am engaged. If I am told a story that I can relate to, now I'm not just engaged; I'm now also a much more captive audience. And, a captive audience is one that is already partially swayed in the direction you want them to go.

Another benefit to storytelling—especially if the story involves you, the storyteller—is that it humanizes you. No longer is your prospect viewing you as a salesperson; now he is viewing you as a person. So, remember to add situational anecdotes to your content, and don't be afraid to show off your humanness.

5. Be consistent

The fifth and final essential area to focus on in your content is *consistency in messaging*. As a business, what you say about your business is either building and supporting your brand, or it is detracting from your brand. The most effective way to ensure you are constantly building your brand is to be consistent in your messaging.

As a business owner, you already know you need to determine what makes your business different, special, and unique. Once those features are defined, you must communicate them…often.

As I have mentioned several times throughout this book, your business's website can be your greatest (and most cost-effective) marketing tool. So, view it as you would a brochure: make sure it contains the most influential information about your business, and make sure everything you say about your business is consistent with your brand. Essentially, you are telling your prospects what they need to hear, and you are doing it repetitively.

Many websites put way too much information on the home page. This can cause your *verbal* message to become confused. (This mistake is quite common, by the way; many business owners have not narrowed down their key messages, and they feel they need to put every single thought they've ever had on the website's homepage).

When there is too much content on the homepage of a website (or any page, for that matter), visitors can easily become confused, which is the opposite of what you want their experience to be. If you have a lot of information to present, one strategy is to use an introduction at the top to clarify and unify the message. In general, however, too much content makes the brand message unclear.

The next website is one that was done right. Right off the bat, there is one simple, direct question that makes the product benefits and target market very clear. The message is succinct, the solution is evident, and the conversion from prospect to customer very likely.

Design © 2011 Cumulus Consulting. All rights reserved.

Action steps

Now that we have fully covered the importance of building a website correctly from the verbal perspective, let's get into the action steps you can take to make a verbally effective website a reality for your business.

The following steps are really questions you will need to ask yourself. So, take out a piece of paper (one sheet for each question), and write down the following questions. Allow yourself to brainstorm, and then narrow down your answers until you are done.

1. What do I want?

2. What do I bring/offer?

3. Who are my audiences? What would they be searching for to find me?

4. What are some anecdotal stories I know of people who have experienced a particular challenge that my type of product/service has helped?

5. If I had to pick one asset of this business that serves the need of my audience, what is it? What would be the second and third?

6. What is my call to action? (Examples include calling you, emailing you, making an online purchase, referring someone to your site, etc.)

Often, success in accomplishing something lies in the questions themselves. When you take the action step of answering these questions, you will have the bulk of the fodder you need for developing effective and great website content.

CHAPTER 7

Step Four: Functionality, Functionality, Functionality!

As I have stated multiple times throughout this book, all successful websites are built to accomplish key business and marketing goals. This objective must also be kept in mind from a functionality standpoint, yet unfortunately many times this very basic requirement is forgotten.

In my professional opinion, there is a set of "cardinal rules" that must be followed to ensure your website is built to be effective and functional. I'm going to outline these rules in this chapter so you can build a website that hits the mark functionally.

Rule #1: Be easy to use

It may sound overly simple or blatantly obvious, but a website must be easy to use! You'd be surprised how many websites are difficult—even impossible—to navigate. If you want your site visitors to read what you have to say, engage with your brand, and take the actions you desire, your site absolutely must be simple to use.

When talking about ease of use, I frequently like to reference a fantastic book on web design by Seth Godin called *The Big Red Fez*. In his book, Godin uses the phrase, "Where is the banana?" in reference to training monkeys. What this means is that, when training monkeys, if you want them to find the banana, you must show them where the banana is!

And since a monkey trainer is using the banana to goad the monkey into taking certain actions, clearly those actions won't be taken if the monkey can't even find the banana.

The following is an example of a 'banana' that can't be found. The website you see below is selling chocolate fountains, and yet when you're on this webpage, it is

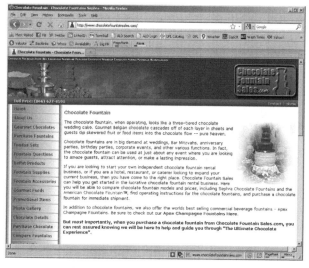

incredibly difficult to know where to go and what to do. The left-side navigation bar has a large number of tabs, and the entire page is overwhelming to look at.

Don't make this mistake! Your website must be functionally designed in a way that makes it clear what you want people to do, and naturally leads them there with ease. Chocolate Fountain Sales has since updated their website with a new e-commerce design that is much easier to navigate.

Rule#2: Intelligent layout

In today's electronic world, people are accessing the Internet from a wide variety of screen types and sizes—from iPods, tablets and Macs to PC laptops and desktops—and the layout of your website must be viewable from all of those which your target customers might be using.

Although a website *should* be designed to look good on the majority of viewing devices, many websites are designed to fit only one size and shape. This issue tends to arise frequently with websites that were built many years ago; since the list of possible viewing devices has exponentially grown, many times an old site design can't be viewed on modern devices.

Here's an example: I was analyzing the website of a client recently, and it turned out her website was designed to fit a 640x480 pixel screen (a standard screen size 10 years ago), yet today the smallest screen size on a desktop PC or laptop is typically 1024x768; and in fact, a lot of websites are optimized for an even larger screen.

The result is that the website does not fill out the screen, which can cause a number of issues. The small size makes the site look dated, for one.

Worse still is the graphic designer with a huge monitor that designs the site to fill their own screen. Here is an example of a website that was designed for a monitor twice as large as the average user's. In this case, the user only sees bits and pieces of the message and the design. The user experience is completely compromised; as you can see, we can only see a fraction of the homepage, and therefore we have no idea what the business does, or what service or product it offers customers.

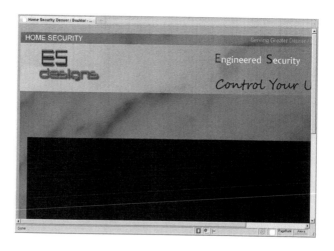

A user can become quickly irritated by having to scroll left and right, up and down…and when that happens, almost 100% of the time, that user leaves the site and goes to find a competing site whose layout makes it easily navigable.

To add insult to injury, this particular home page design consists of a multi-megabyte Flash presentation that fills the home page. Although the graphic designer could say that the large Flash file "played fine" on his own computer, when a user is viewing this site over the Internet, the home page takes several minutes to load!

The moral of the story is that as you embark on building your website, it is critical to consider your target customers and what type of devices will be used to view your website.

Rule #3: Easy site navigation and access

How a business's website is organized is a direct reflection of how organized the business is. When people have a hard time finding what they're looking for on the website, not only are they frustrated with the website, they are frustrated with the business.

A web page should be not just attractive and informative, but it must be directive, as well. A user should have no problem understanding exactly what she is supposed to do, and given an easy way to do it. And yet, many websites—no matter how pretty or well-worded—leave users wondering how to get where they need to go. That's a great way to lose your customers before they're even customers!

In the case of Dell in the example below, it is made very clear what a customer should do. A customer who wants to 'celebrate the holidays with Dell' knows exactly where to click…as does a customer buying

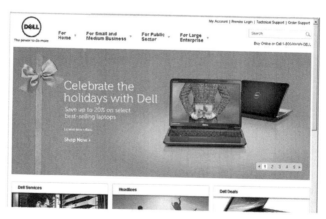

products for the home; a small or medium business; a member of the public sector; or a large enterprise. In addition, the 'search' box is clearly visible.

When visiting this website, it's very easy to navigate, and it's very clear what to do. Its navigation is clean and simple, and it is easily found across the top and in the center of the page. Additionally, access to key information and retail shopping is made simple and quick.

If you do want to get fancy…say, using a flash presentation to engage your users…you need to consider download speed to ensure ease of use for your prospective customers. In many cases, flash presentations can take up to 30 seconds to download (there are a number of factors that can cause this, one of which is the quality of your web host). The point is, be sure that any graphic or video enhancements are an asset, not a deterrent, to your website.

In conclusion to our discussion on hyperlinks and access, my main message is that sometimes less is more. Keep it clean, display navigation bar tabs clearly, and make access to information and actions easy.

Rule #4: Use hyperlinks wisely

Hyperlinks are essential for ensuring your visitors can quickly and easily jump from page to page as needed. It follows, then, that by clearly formatting hyperlinks, you make it easier for users to navigate your site—and that's important. Why? Because if visitors don't know how to navigate your site, they won't.

One issue I often come across is that it is not always apparent to the user which elements are hyperlinks, and which are not. In the case of many websites (especially ones that were built many years ago), some pages have bold or bold/underlined text that appears to be a hyperlink but is not.

Another danger is having images which are hyperlinked, but which don't have text associated with them. In other words, when a user hovers over an image but no text pops up, the user doesn't necessarily know to click on it, since it's not clearly distinguished as a hyperlink.

Another common concern I see with hyperlinking is when hyperlinks *don't work*. I almost want to say, "enough said" here, but it's such an epidemic that I must address it further. If you go look through 10 websites in their entirety, I'll bet that eight of them have broken link issues, or links that dead end or link to the wrong page. From a functional standpoint, hyperlinks—*all of them*—must work flawlessly, without exception.

Action steps

As you can tell, having a website that is functionally effective is critical. We have covered the main areas to consider in ensuring that functionality is in place in this chapter; now let's cover some steps you can take to get you on the path to creating a functionally sound website.

1. When you go to build a website, make sure you are clear that it must be easy to use, above all else. This will mean that you need to be involved in understanding the site mapping and plans for navigation.

2. Plan carefully with your graphic designer how the layout is going to look. Make sure it is very obvious what you want your visitors to do once they get to your website; 'show them the banana!'

3. Use common sense when you go to create accessibility and build navigation bar tabs out. The navigation bar tabs should be self-explanatory and clearly direct visitors to the other pages. Try to put yourself in the shoes of your user: what would you need to see in order to get where you need to go?

4. Be smart about incorporating hyperlinks throughout your web pages. Be critical when you beta test your site, and make sure each and every hyperlink works, leads users where it is supposed to, and is clearly marked as a hyperlink.

The best way to ensure that your website functions seamlessly is to keep everything we've discussed in mind, and be meticulous about making sure everything is user friendly…and that everything works the way it should.

CHAPTER 8

Step Five: Let's Speak "Geek": Technical Aspects of a Great Website

A website is not a good website unless it's well-designed technically. It's as simple as that.

What do I mean by "technically?" When I speak of the technical aspect of websites, this includes all the back-end detail, from hosting to code to meta-tags. And, yes, this is where we get into the computer nerd-isms that are rarely understood by people who don't "speak geek." That's why you're reading this book!

Imagine your website is a sports car. It may be the best-looking sports car in town, but what actually makes it go fast? The answer is not the killer paint job or the chrome wheels…it's what happens under the hood. In this chapter, we're going to get into "what's under the hood" of your website, because without this, a website is nothing but some pictures and words on a page.

First let's talk about what makes up a website. In essence, a website is a collection of text files containing some code, and some media files and pictures sitting on a computer somewhere. It might have a nice design, and it may even boast the best written content in the land, but what is going on behind all that?

What gives your website real traction—what makes it optimized for the best-possible chance of being found by the right people (a phenomenon otherwise referred to as Search Engine Optimization, or "SEO")—is what goes on under the hood. These are the technical, invisible elements that you don't see, but that make a huge impact on your website's success.

> *The quality of a person's life*
> *is directly proportional*
> *to their commitment to excellence,*
> *regardless of their chosen field of endeavor.*
>
> **– Vince Lombardi**

In this chapter I'm going to cover the essential elements of a technically sound website for maximum SEO.

HTML/CSS code

You've probably heard of code, but you likely haven't heard it described in terms of why, exactly, it's important. In a nutshell, the HTML and CSS code used on a website affects the site's performance, both in terms of user experience and search engine rankings. When it comes to writing code, the primary goal...and this may sound so reasonable that it's confusing...is that it is readable.

That's right—search engines are just like us: they want readable content, readable code!

So, what's the difference between good code and bad code?

Let's talk about bad code first. Bad code looks like gibberish. Many times this is the type of code that is generated by the hundreds of DIY, "make your own website" offerings out there. You see, search engines don't look at web pages; they look at website code.

For example, Google at its core is a text matching machine—its job is to match what you type in the search engine with what's on the page.

When a search engine looks at a bunch of bad code, it sees exactly what you would see: nonsense. What does that do? The page will never show up in search results, because no one's search could possibly match the gibberish.

Here is an example of the gibberish I'm describing. This is what it looks like when viewing the source code in the browser window:

```html
<body bgcolor="#ffffff" background="img/base/bg.jpg">
<!-- imageready slices (1039.2.psd) -->
<table id="table_01" width="1000" border="0"
cellpadding="0" cellspacing="0" align="center"
style="border-right:1px solid #000000; border-left:1px
solid #000000;" background="img/base/bgtile.html">
<tr>
<td rowspan="2" valign="top">
<img alt="" id="ba51" src="img/base/ba51.jpg"
width="130" height="97" alt="" /></td>
    <td colspan="7" valign="top">
<!--Tempdesignbeginmt--><img alt="" id="akmtitle"
id="akmtitle" src="img/titles/mt.jpg" width="611"
height="68" alt="" /><!--Tempdesignendmt--></td>
    <td colspan="3" valign="top">
      <img alt="" id="ba52" src="img/base/ba52.jpg"
width="259" height="68" alt="" /></td>
  </tr>
  <tr>
    <td colspan="5" valign="top">
      <img alt="" id="ba53" src="img/base/ba53.jpg"
width="311" height="29" alt="" /></td>
```

You probably can't read this. Guess what? Neither can Google! Now, let's look at a sample of good code:

```
<div id="content-wrapper">
   <div id="column-1">
       <h1>Make your auction event </h1>
      <h2>the most eagerly anticipated,<br />
          extraordinary celebration<br />
          of the year</h2>
   </div>
   <div id="column-2">
       <div id="hp-2b">
          <p>What if you could connect your auction
guests to your cause in such a special way that your event
becomes the most anticipated, well-attended fundraising
party of the year? </p>
          <p>When you hire auctioneer and event producer
Brad Kinney, that's exactly what happens.  Suddenly, what
was to be an ordinary auction becomes an extraordinary
celebration.</p>
       </div>
   </div>
   <div class="clear-float"></div>
   <div id="column-1">
      <h3>Brad brings your event to life<br />
      like no one else.</h3>
```

This is an example of what good website code looks like. It is easy to read; most of it is in plain English, and you can read it. Guess what? So can the search engines.

The bottom line is, good code is readable to both humans and machines, so the way your code is written is critical to your success in being found online.

Overnight visibility

Not long ago, I met a travel agent who was frustrated by her website's performance. When meeting with her, I learned that she had been paying a major national company—the same company that built her website—to do "search engine optimization" for the past 9 months—with no results.

In fact, when I dove a little deeper, I discovered that her web pages had not even been indexed by Google; i.e., it was impossible for her to show up in search results, because *her pages didn't even exist in Google's database*! This was particularly frustrating because she was targeting a small niche in the travel industry, and after 9 months of *real* SEO work, should have dominated the search results.

We proposed a simple solution—without changing her web design, we rewrote the underlying HTML code, and moved her site to another web host (more on web hosting later in this chapter).

Within a week of the changes, she was showing up on page 2 of Google search results for her targeted terms, and by the second week, she was showing up on page 1.

Titles and meta tags

If you've ever had a website built, created one yourself, or discussed having one built, you have probably heard the term "meta tags." And, if you're like most people, these are two words that make your eyes glaze over. I'm asking you now to open your eyes back up, and hear me out, because once meta tags are understood, you'll find them neither boring nor expendable.

Essentially, meta tags are descriptions which are embedded in the headers of web pages. Website visitors do not see meta tags, but they are used to provide key information to the search engines. Even more simply explained, meta tags tell search engines what the web page is all about; so you can see why meta tags are critically important to your success in effective SEO.

Closely related to the meta tags is the page title. This too does not show up "on screen," but it is one of the most important elements for your Google ranking.

So, what is a good title or meta tag? Well, titles and meta tags should align with terms your users are searching for. As an example, I recently worked with a client who used the following as a page title and meta

tag for a Denver-based charity's website: "About us."
Now, I ask you: how many people are using the term
"About us" to search for a Denver-based charity? I
think you know the answer.

Instead of using generic search terms, you want
your titles and keyword meta tags to include words
which are actually used on the page—they should
reflect the content on the page. In fact, if they don't, the
search engines may not include your website in their
search results, even when it would make sense to find
you otherwise.

This does not mean you should stuff a bunch of
keywords into the meta tags. If the keywords listed in
your meta tag are not words you are actually using in
your page content, it can result in a penalty with some
of the search engines, causing them to stop including
your pages in search results.

In the past few years, because so many people
have abused meta tags in an attempt to manipulate the
search engines, Google has stopped factoring the most
common meta tags into their search results. However,
the page's title tag continues to be one of the most
important ranking factors on the page.

Make them unique

An important principle in using title tags effectively is to ensure that each web page has a different title. The same is true if you are editing the meta tags—especially the meta description. This is a mistake that is very commonly made when website are built: using the same titles, descriptions and tags on all the pages of the site.

If I had to summarize, I would say that in order to ensure you're using page titles and meta tags to your advantage, you need to:

- Select appropriate keywords for each page to target
- Write a unique, descriptive page title for each page
- Include targeted keywords in page titles
- If you use the meta description tag, write a useful and unique page description for the page
- Only list keywords in your keyword meta tag that you actually use on the page.

Keywords

One of the main factors that determine the success of your search engine optimization campaign—and your website—is the group of keywords that you choose to target. You want to ensure that as you choose the keywords you will weave throughout the website content on all your pages, you keep several important things in mind. I will cover those now.

First of all, identify what your potential customer is actually looking for. (There's not much point in ranking first for a term that no one searches on! All successful SEO and PPC campaigns start with some analysis of your online market, so that you can design a meaningful strategy.)

Secondly, look for underserved or overlooked niches in your marketplace based on competition, search volume, and market opportunities for each keyword.

In defining keywords, you also need to be specific, and make sure each word relates to your topic or business. Many websites make the mistake of being too broad, general or ambiguous, which impedes the success of your SEO.

You also want to be aware of terms that face an extremely high level of competition. Examples of this might be, "doctor," "insurance," "lawyer," etc. Now,

I admit this is easier said than done…but a good SEO expert will be able to help determine the best ways to choose the keywords that maximize your opportunities.

Hosting

For many people, choosing where their website is hosted comes down to one simple thing: cost. I can say right off the bat, choosing where your site is hosted on price alone is a huge mistake.

The fact is, where your website is hosted makes a difference. I'm going to get into the how and why behind that in minute, but first let's discuss what happens when someone pulls up your URL.

Here's the simple version: When someone clicks on your URL or types it into their browser, their computer reaches out to a DNS server, which is essentially a phone book…a directory of where websites live. It then retrieves the IP address of the computer, or server, that your website is sitting on, and it then goes to that web host to request the files that constitute your web page.

Now let's get back to that area where your website is hosted, and why it matters. The vast majority of websites are hosted on a server that is hosting dozens, hundreds, even thousands of websites. I'm going to refer to that area in which your site and those hosted with it "live" as a "neighborhood." Now, there are good neighborhoods and there are bad neighborhoods. And it really, really matters which one your website lives in.

No Free Lunch

Watch out for web hosting providers that offer "unlimited" services, such as unlimited disk space, unlimited bandwidth, etc. Disk space, bandwidth, and CPU cycles cost the hosting company money. Therefore, the only way a hosting company can be successful offering "unlimited" services is if all their customers are not! There's no such thing as a free lunch.

A buffet restaurant can offer "all-you-can-eat" because there is a limit to how much any person can eat in one sitting. A successful website, though, can use 100,000 times the bandwidth than that of a failed website. Know this for certain: If your website becomes successful and starts to use a lot of resources, the "unlimited" hosting provider will ask you to upgrade or simply shut down your site. And, meanwhile, the rate-limited service will hurt your chances of being successful in the first place.

Best advice: Pay more for a hosting service that provides a fixed amount of disk space and bandwidth that is all yours to use, like this one from Cumulus Consulting: http://number1employee.com/services/web-hosting/

I'm going to use a real-life analogy to illustrate why this matters and how it impacts how your website is treated. Many years ago, I lived with my wife in Anaheim, California and I was doing some non-profit volunteer work. I didn't make a large income, and we lived in a small apartment…not much to speak of. One day we had a break-in, and when the police arrived to investigate, we found ourselves being interrogated, rather than being treated with respect and helpfulness.

A year later, I had transitioned back into the biotech industry, and we bought a house about a mile away from the apartment, in a much more affluent neighborhood. While living there, my car got broken into, and when the police arrived on the scene, they bent over backwards to provide protection, safety and comfort.

What caused the police to treat us so vastly different in each scenario was clear. It was our neighborhood. They made assumptions about us, and acted differently, due to assumptions they made about the neighborhood we lived in.

The same goes for search engines. They choose how to "treat" your website in large part based on where it "lives." The truth is that to be treated well, you need to be in good company, in a good neighborhood, with good neighbors. You can imagine there are a wide range of types of website neighbors: do you want your site to live next to a website containing explicit language or graphics, a website that has malware, or a "spam" site? Trust me: you don't.

You also want to consider the number of neighbors you have in your host neighborhood. There is an area of my city where a lot of housing has been recently developed, and there's only one major service street in and out of that area. The traffic in the mornings is horrendous!

It's the same with your website. Your site can be on a computer with 3,000 other websites, 10,000 other websites, or you can be on a computer with 5 other websites. Have you ever had 20 programs open on your computer and everything starts to slow down? That's essentially what happens when there is too much hosted on one server. How much faster and more responsive is your website going to be if there is a smaller number on that server? The answer is, much faster. And that speed of retrieving your site directly impacts your users' experience on your website.

When a search engine indexes your site, they will pull up all of your web pages in a few seconds. If your server can't handle the load, the search engine will simply go away and try again some other time… maybe. Having a web host that offers *dedicated* resources to serving up your web pages goes a long way toward helping you get a good ranking on Google.

Action steps

When you go about building your website, you must prioritize making it technically effective at its very foundation. If you don't, the rest hardly matters. Take the following steps as you go about creating your website.

Make sure your HTML code is readable to humans. That's the best way to ensure it will be readable to the search engines.

Refer back to the discussion on title tags and meta tags in this chapter. The rule of thumb is, make sure your title tags and meta tags relate to the actual content on your website, and don't be repetitive page after page. Each page's content is unique, and your titles and meta tags should reflect that.

Regarding keywords, the main message is, choose your words carefully! Again, refer to the tips administered in this chapter: you must work with someone who knows how to choose keywords, and/or become educated on key word research yourself.

Remember that "where you live" matters. Choose where your website is hosted carefully, because it matters.

Now you've been versed in what it means to have a technically sound website. This knowledge, if used, is powerful. I hope this has dispelled some myths and solved some mysteries. In moving forward, it's simply a matter of sticking to the action steps, and applying what you now know—so you can create a website capable of making money for your business.

Putting It All to Work

Now we've seen that you can have a website that actually makes you money, that returns much, much more than you invest in it, and that functions as your Number 1 Employee. Regardless of your experience in the past, it is possible to have a website that works for you to make you money as long as you apply the 5-steps presented in this book.

It starts with clearly defining your business **purpose** for your website—what do you want your website to do for you to grow the business?

Then, it's as simple as following the formula for website success:

- Strong **visual** design that communicates your brand and personality and makes people want to do business with you;

- Great **verbal** messages that catch people's attention and get them to take action;

- A **functional** design that creates a great user experience and gently leads people where you want them to go;

- And the **technical**, "under-the-hood" aspects such as good code, SEO, and high-quality web hosting.

If you have a dream of having your website working for you 24/7 to grow your business, you now have a clear road map to get there.

If you want something
you have never had,
be prepared
to do something
you have never done.

We know that this formula works, because we have clients who use it every day to get huge benefits, and we have seen it work for hundreds of websites.

The fastest way to get started
is simply to get started.

Take action now

The fastest way to get started is simply to get started. Here are some simple action steps you can take to get you moving in this process. When you work with us, we will spend dozens of hours to help you find the ideal answers to these questions, but you can also work through them on your own.

1. Decide whom you're targeting

Before you design a website, you must know who your target client is. When I speak at a business convention, whether it be a keynote address or a breakout session, business owners often say to me, "Steve, how can I work with you?" Because I have to be selective about who I work with, I have developed a clear profile of what my target client looks like. My ideal prospect is a business owner or senior level manager responsible for business growth. In addition, I am looking for people like this:

- Have an established business that provides a full-time income

- You strongly desire to have a website that functions as your #1 employee

- You are tired of having a website that does little for your business, and would like a website that really makes you money

- You are willing to invest in your business in order to have it grow

- You are willing to devote some time to the consulting process so that we can develop a customized marketing strategy

- You or your staff are willing to provide input into your website's content, up front and potentially on an ongoing basis

- You don't want to spend your time managing your website

- You want the absolute best people in the industry to build and manage your website for you

Since we have this profile in mind, we do not need our website to appeal to people who are thinking about starting a business, who are converting their hobby into a business, or who are satisfied with their current level of income and have no desire to grow. We can focus all our energy on appealing to the right client.

My ideal client is:

_____

_____

_____

_____

2. Determine your website's goals

Once you know who your target client is, you then need to determine what your website can and should do to help you grow the business. Website goals vary greatly from business to business. Here are some examples of valid website goals.

- For an *engineering firm*, to get prospective clients to pick up the phone and call.

- For a *golf supply store*, to sell products online.

- For an *orthodontist*, to get prospective patients to book an appointment for an initial consultation.

- For an *author/speaker/info marketer*, to build a tribe of followers that will be eager to buy additional materials.

- For a *photographer*, to showcase their work so that prospective clients will be convinced to hire.

- For a *commercial printer*, to generate leads or requests for a quote.

- For a *restaurant*, to provide location and hours, menus, testimonials, and to allow online reservations and takeout orders.

- For a *data service*, to add online subscribers.

These are just a few simple examples. The possibilities and combinations are endless, but there are probably only a few goals that are the best use of the website for *your* business.

My website's goals are:

To target people who like an organic lifestyle. From food to skin + body care

3. Who are you competing against?

Two men were lying in their sleeping bags in a tent when they saw a bear come crashing toward their camp site.

One man immediately started running
away, while his companion pulled on
his boots and began lacing them up.

"What are you doing?"
the man shouted to his friend.
"You can't outrun the bear!"

"I don't have to,"
his friend shouted back.
"I just have to outrun you!"

When we are building a website that will be your number 1 employee, we invest a lot of time in studying the industry and your competition. This tells us two things. (1) What are the current trends and design styles in the industry, and (2) What do we have to do to create a site that will blow away all your competition?

When you look around at your competition, think about what will set your site apart from your competitors. Also notice what some of them are doing that might be a great idea that you can adopt.

My website will be outstanding when:

_____

_____

_____

_____

4. Hire the right company to build your website

It is impossible for one person to be really good at visual design, branding, developing key marketing messages, writing compelling copy, designing the site's user experience, coding the site, performing search engine optimization, and developing the campaigns to bring potential customers to your site. A team approach is always the best approach for building a website.

It is also very hard to go out and hire a designer, copy writer, programmers, etc., and expect them to work cohesively to bring about a great end product. A good team has a strong leader who keeps everyone focused on the goal—a website that will make money for you. The members of a good team understand that achieving that goal is much more important that merely being good at their individual craft. And with a good team, the value is always much more than the sum of the parts.

As I was writing this chapter, I was talking to a friend who is currently involved in a major website project that is coming unglued. The client had hired a great marketing expert from Chicago to write the copy, a terrific designer from Texas, an excellent programmer from Ohio, and an SEO company from another part of the country. Each one of the vendors is good at what they do, but no one is in charge to make sure the website sticks to its primary goal. And there is no one who is really able to mediate between the conflicting demands of say, the copy writer and the SEO guy, or the designer and the coder. This project is like a car without a driver!

When you are hiring someone to build your website for you, it is helpful to be very clear what criteria you will use to select the firm. Be sure you hire someone who tailors the website to your business goals. Here's a good rule of thumb: If you ask someone to build you a website, and they simply say, "Okay," then that's probably not someone you want to hire! A good firm will spend a lot of time understanding your business and your goals before they start in on a project.

Also, when you hire a web firm, don't just look at the design portfolio. Obviously, if their designs are terrible, you don't want to hire them, but a good firm can produce designs in many different styles. *Their mindset about how the website can benefit your business is much more important than the styles of designs they have created for other clients.* Your business is unique, so your web design should also be unique.

My web company needs to:

_____

_____

_____

5. Plan your follow-up campaign

The best time to think about how you will get people to the website is before the website is ever built. What strategies will you use to bring people to your site?

When we work with you as our client, we do not want to build a site and then leave you on your own— "high and dry" so to speak. We also do not want to build you a 50 foot bridge across a 60 foot river. To us, a website project is the start of an ongoing partnership, with the goal of making you money and growing your business.

For some types of businesses, social media may be a great medium to do that. For other types of businesses, social media may not be that effective. For most businesses, some level of search engine optimization will be necessary to maximize your website's earning potential. Understanding who your target client is and their online shopping habits will go a long way toward determining how you will "market" your website.

The top ways I can bring people to my site are:

_____

_____

_____

_____

The most important thing is to begin.
Fear of failure can immobilize you,
even with a great idea....
Fear of failure paralyzes people
and makes failure certain.

– Dan Miller

6. Who will manage your campaign?

Lastly, make sure you know *who* is going to manage your website and execute your well-thought-out marketing campaigns. The best plan will not work if you don't have the right people in place to follow it! Some companies like to manage this in-house, but most of our clients prefer to have an outside professional firm manage this for them. They also find that they usually get better results that way!

A Note from Steve

Congratulations for investing in yourself by reading *Five Easy Steps to Make Your Website Your #1 Employee*! I hope this book has helped you think about your website in new ways.

If this book is helpful to you and you want to continue it, then sign up for my free email *Successful Online Marketing*. You'll receive a short weekly email with additional marketing ideas and tips that my clients have found helpful.

As a thank-you bonus, I invite you to download and experience my audio program, *How to Make Your Website Your #1 Employee*. This is a program that I have presented to thousands of business owners with great results.

You can sign up for both at either 5StepsBook.com or Number1Employee.com.

Also, if you enjoyed this book, please help other readers find it too:

1. This book is lendable, so send it to a friend who you think might like it so he or she can discover me, too.

2. Help other people find this book by writing a review.

3. Sign up to be notified of new releases by contacting me at Number1Employee.com so you can find out about the next book as soon as it's available.

4. Come like my Facebook page, Facebook.com/CumulusConsulting.

5. Connect with me on Facebook and LinkedIn.

LinkedIn.com/in/SEJohnsen

Facebook.com/SEJohnsen

If you would like to share how this book has made a difference in your business and in your life, please write to me. I am always excited when my readers share what has been most valuable to them, or when I have the privilege of hearing your personal stories.

Number1Employee.com

www.Cumulus-Consulting.com

Together with my team at Cumulus Consulting, I wish you all the best in your journey!

To your success,

Steve Johnsen

Free Bonus Resources

We have worked hard to provide as many resources as possible to support you in your business growth.

Business and marketing tips

Free! Occasional marketing & business tips sent out by email (sign up at 5StepsBook.com/Free)

Free! Daily marketing tips, business tips, and inspiring quotes delivered on Facebook and Twitter:

@TheCumulus

Facebook.com/CumulusConsulting

Free podcast

To download a free podcast presenting the concepts in this book, just visit 5StepsBook.com/Free.

Free e-book

To download a *free* copy of Steve Johnsen's popular e-book, *A Website is Like a Poem*, go to

5StepsBook.com/Free

$50 credit voucher

To receive a $50 credit voucher good toward your investment in the *Power Strategies for Making Your Website Your #1 Employee* home study course, simply visit

5StepsBook.com/CreditVoucher

and enter this code to receive your discount: **5esbd**

Sample program

To receive a sample audio program from the *Power Strategies for Making Your Website Your #1 Employee* home study course, contact the author on his website:

Number1Employee.com

www.Cumulus-Consulting.com

About the Author

Steve Johnsen, MBA, is a public speaker, author, business consultant, coach and technology expert who has spent his career serving as a leading authority on business growth.

After working for more than 25 years in high-level leadership positions turning around companies, he now couples his unparalleled understanding of web technology with ingenious business strategy to create websites that actually make money for businesses. Johnsen lives in the Denver, Colorado metro area and can be reached at www.steve-johnsen.com.

If you enjoyed Five Easy Steps to Make Your Website Your #1 Employee,

Steve Johnsen is the ideal professional speaker for your next event!

"The Website Income Strategist"

Steve Johnsen is one of the country's premier technology and business-building experts, and is recognized by his clients and colleagues as a business and marketing "genius." Well-known for his business/technology seminars and boot camps, he is also the very successful founder of Cumulus Consulting, a firm dedicated to helping businesses use their websites to make them money. He has 30 years of experience in technology, as well as more than 20 years successfully building and turning around businesses. As an International speaker, author, and business coach, he is helping businesses grow by bringing together the best practices in both technology and business.

Steve's seminars inspire people to think strategically about their website so that their website can become their most effective salesperson.

Steve's most requested and popular programs

How to Make Your Website Your #1 Employee (tailored to your group)

Leadership at the Speed of Twitter

3 Keys to Making Money and Getting Real Customers through Social Media

If you would like to know more about booking Steve for a keynote address, breakout session, or group workshop, please contact Cumulus Consulting at 303-335-0949.

Share this book!

Quantity discounts of this book are available. Contact the publisher at CentennialPublishing.com for more information.

This book may also be ordered through Ingram or NACSCORP, on Amazon.com, through Barnes & Noble (in-store or online at barnesandnoble.com), or through your local book store.

18278077R00084

Made in the USA
San Bernardino, CA
07 January 2015